traditional irish cooking

This edition published by Parragon Books Ltd in 2013 and distributed by

Parragon Inc.
440 Park Avenue South, 13th Floor
New York, NY 10016
www.parragon.com/lovefood

LOVE FOOD is an imprint of Parragon Books Ltd

Copyright © Parragon Books Ltd 2009–2013

LOVE FOOD and the accompanying heart device is a registered trademark of Parragon Books Ltd in the USA, the UK, Australia, India, and the EU.

All rights reserved. No part of this publication may be reproduced, stored in a retrieval system, or transmitted, in any form or by any means, electric, mechanical, photocopying, recording, or otherwise, without the prior permission of the copyright holder.

ISBN 978-1-4723-3006-2

Printed in China

Cover image by Mike Cooper

Notes for the Reader
This book uses standard kitchen measuring spoons and cups. All spoon and cup measurements are level unless otherwise indicated. Unless otherwise stated, milk is assumed to be whole, eggs are large, individual vegetables are medium, and pepper is freshly ground black pepper. Unless otherwise stated, all root vegetables should be washed in plain water and peeled prior to using.

For best results, use a food thermometer when cooking meat and poultry. Check the latest USDA government guidelines for current advice.

Garnishes, decorations, and serving suggestions are all optional and not necessarily included in the recipe ingredients or method. The times given are only an approximate guide. Preparation times differ according to the techniques used by different people and the cooking times may also vary from those given. Optional ingredients, variations, or serving suggestions have not been included in the time calculations.

Recipes using raw or very lightly cooked eggs should be avoided by infants, the elderly, pregnant women, convalescents, and anyone with a weakened immune system. Pregnant and breast-feeding women are advised to avoid eating peanuts and peanut products. People with nut allergies should be aware that some of the prepared ingredients used in the recipes in this book may contain nuts. Always check the packaging before use.

Picture Acknowledgments
The publisher would like to thank Getty Images for permission to reproduce copyright material on the following pages: 5, 7, 13, 19, 22, 26, 37, 38, 49 & 53.

Contents

	Introduction	4
Chapter 1	Appetizers & Snacks	6
Chapter 2	Mains	18
Chapter 3	Sides	36
Chapter 4	Desserts	52
	Index	64

Introduction

Irish food has come a long way in recent years and traditional Irish pubs have also become great places to eat. A new generation of exciting young chefs has transformed Irish food, creating new dishes and giving a twist to many of the classic favorites. This collection brings together the best of the old and new. It includes classics like Skink Soup, Dublin Coddle, Irish Stew, and Soda Bread. There are also exciting contemporary dishes such as Buttermilk Pancakes, Roasted Banana Shallots, and Chocolate & Stout Ice Cream.

The Irish also love their savoury pies—hot, warm or cold, eaten at home, in a restaurant, or outdoors. They come with a variety of tasty fillings and toppings. This collection includes three classics that have also been adapted to fit this traditional Irish pie pan. All the variations serve two people.

Beef & Stout Pies (page 20) are an all-time favorite, combining tender meat with richly flavored stout gravy and topped with light puff pastry.

Fisherman's Pie (page 24) brings together the best of Irish seafood with a delicious creamy mashed potato topping.

The Potato, Leek & Chicken Pie (page 28) is a modern take on a traditional favorite that uses crispy phyllo pastry above a tasty filling—perfect for a summer's day because it is light and not at all stodgy.

So whatever dish you choose, this book will bring you a true taste of Ireland.

Included on the back of this pack are cardboard shamrock-shaped stencils. Cut them out, trace around them onto parchment paper and use the parchment paper stencils to create shapes with pastry. Ensure that the cardboard stencils do not come into direct contact with food.

Chapter 1
APPETIZERS & SNACKS

Irish Buttermilk Pancakes

Nothing goes to waste in the Irish kitchen, including buttermilk: the thin liquid left over after churning butter. It has a pleasing, tangy flavor and is a main ingredient in Irish baking. Similar to drop biscuits in thickness, buttermilk pancakes have a slightly crisp, golden crust, and a fluffy center.

Makes 12

1 1/3 cups all-purpose flour
3/4 tablespoon sugar
1/2 teaspoon salt
1 teaspoon baking soda
1 egg, lightly beaten
1 1/2 cups buttermilk
3 tablespoons vegetable oil, plus extra for brushing

To serve
2/3 cup heavy cream, whipped
1 cup blueberries

- Sift the flour, sugar, salt, and baking soda into a mixing bowl.

- Mix the egg with the buttermilk and vegetable oil in a large pitcher. Add to the dry ingredients, beating to a smooth, creamy batter. Let stand for at least 30 minutes or up to 2 hours.

- Heat a nonstick skillet or flat griddle pan over medium heat and brush with vegetable oil. Pour in enough batter to make 4-inch circles (about 1/4 cup per pancake). Cook for 1 1/2–2 minutes per side, or until small bubbles appear on the surface. Remove to a dish and keep warm while you cook the rest.

- Serve with softly whipped cream and blueberries.

Skink Soup

"Skink" is an old Irish and Scots term meaning "broth." This version, sometimes called Irish chicken soup, is made with diced chicken and colorful summer vegetables, enriched with cream and egg yolk. Although lighter than traditional winter broths, it still makes a satisfying meal-in-a-bowl.

Serves 4

2 celery stalks, halved lengthwise and diced
4 small carrots, thinly sliced
1 small leek, halved lengthwise and sliced
3½ cups chicken stock
1 bay leaf
1 cup diced cooked chicken
½ cup shelled peas
4 small scallions, some green tops included, sliced
1 egg yolk
⅓ cup heavy whipping cream
4 Boston or butter lettuce leaves, shredded
salt and pepper

❈ Put the celery, carrots, and leek in a saucepan with the stock, bay leaf, and salt and pepper to taste. Cover and bring to a boil. Reduce the heat to medium, then simmer for 15 minutes, or until tender.

❈ Add the chicken, peas, and scallions. Simmer for about 8 minutes, or until the peas are just tender.

❈ Remove the pan from the heat. Lightly beat the egg yolk and cream together, and stir the mixture into the soup. Reheat gently, stirring.

❈ Ladle into warm bowls, add the lettuce, and serve immediately.

Irish Rarebit

Meaning "tasty morsel," "rarebit" (or "rabbit") is a popular light course throughout Ireland and the British Isles, where it is traditionally served at "high tea." Numerous recipes exist, but most include cheese and mustard. Rarebit is delicious on toasted Irish soda bread, topped with chopped pickles.

Serves 4

2 cups shredded mild cheddar cheese
2 tablespoons lightly salted butter
¼ cup whole milk
1 teaspoon cider vinegar
1 teaspoon dry mustard
4 slices whole-wheat or soda bread
2 tablespoons chopped dill pickles
salt and pepper

✛ Preheat the broiler until hot. Put the cheese, butter, and milk in a saucepan and heat gently, stirring, until creamy and smooth. Add the vinegar, mustard, and seasoning to the sauce.

✛ Toast the bread on one side only. Place on a baking sheet, with the uncooked side facing upward. Pour the sauce over the bread. Place under the preheated broiler for 2–3 minutes, until golden and bubbling.

✛ Sprinkle with the chopped pickles and serve immediately.

GLENOE VILLAGE, COUNTY ANTRIM

Kipper & Potato Salad with Mustard Dressing

Made with gutted and split herrings smoked over oak chips, kippers are one of Ireland's best-loved cured fish. Their tasty dense, brown flesh is excellent eaten raw in a salad, as in this recipe, but it is also good broiled or briefly boiled in water.

Serves 4–6

1½ pounds waxy new potatoes, scrubbed
3 tablespoons chopped fresh dill, plus sprigs to garnish
4 scallions, some green tops included, diagonally sliced
8 radishes, sliced
4 kipper fillets, about 2½ ounces each
salt

Mustard dressing
1 teaspoon dry mustard
pinch of sugar
salt and pepper
2 tablespoons cider vinegar
2 tablespoons heavy cream
3 tablespoons peanut oil
3 tablespoons olive oil

- Cook the potatoes in boiling salted water for 15–20 minutes, or until just tender. Drain and slice widthwise into ¼-inch pieces. Set aside to cool.

- To make the dressing, combine the mustard, sugar, salt and pepper, cider vinegar, and heavy cream. Gradually add the oils, whisking until smooth and thick.

- Put the potatoes in a bowl, and mix with the dressing and dill. Add most of the scallions and radishes, reserving a few to garnish. Check the seasoning, and add more salt and pepper if necessary.

- Remove the skin from the kipper fillets. Slice each fillet lengthwise into four, then slice each piece widthwise into thin bite-size strips.

- Divide the potato mixture among individual serving plates. Arrange the kipper strips attractively on top, and garnish with the reserved scallions, radishes, and dill sprigs.

Bacon, Beet & Spinach Salad with Cashel Blue Cheese

Cashel Blue cheese is made near the Rock of Cashel in County Tipperary. When mature, it develops a mellow, slightly spicy flavor that goes well with beets. A good alternative would be a traditional farmhouse hard blue cheese such as Maytag Blue.

Serves 4–6

10–12 small beets, no more than 2 inches in diameter
6 bacon strips
4 cups baby spinach
6 ounces Cashel Blue cheese, broken into small chunks
1/3 cup toasted hazelnuts
2 tablespoons chopped chives

Dressing

1 shallot, finely chopped
2 teaspoons white wine vinegar
1 teaspoon Dijon mustard
salt and pepper
1/3 cup extra virgin olive oil

- Preheat the broiler to high. Trim all but 1/2 inch of stem from the beets and any long roots. Leave the peel in place. Plunge into a large saucepan of boiling water, bring back to a boil, then simmer briskly for about 30 minutes, or until the beets are just tender. Drain and let cool a little.

- Meanwhile, broil the bacon for 4–5 minutes, turning once, until crisp. Blot with paper towels and slice widthwise into bite-size pieces. Set aside and keep warm.

- Whisk together the dressing ingredients in a pitcher and set aside.

- When the beets are cool enough to handle, remove the peel, leaving the stem in place and being careful to avoid damaging the flesh. Using a sharp knife, slice the beets in half lengthwise.

- Arrange the spinach leaves on a serving platter or individual plates. Whisk the dressing again and spoon a little over the leaves. Arrange the beets attractively on top and pour the remaining dressing over them. Scatter with the cheese, bacon, and nuts, finishing with a sprinkling of chives.

Chapter 2
MAINS

Beef & Stout Pies

TO USE YOUR PIE PAN
Follow the recipe with these changes: use only 1 tablespoon all-purpose flour and half quantities of all the other ingredients. Spoon the cooked meat mixture and all the gravy into the pie pan and top with the pastry. Bake for 15–20 minutes at 425°F until the pastry is risen and golden.

Serves 4

3 tablespoons all-purpose flour
1 teaspoon salt
½ teaspoon black pepper
2 pounds boneless chuck steak or eye of round steak, cut into 1-inch pieces
vegetable oil, for frying
1¼ cups meat stock
1 onion, coarsely chopped
8 ounces cremini mushrooms, stems discarded, caps quartered
1 tablespoon tomato paste
2 teaspoons chopped fresh thyme
1 cup stout
1 pound store-bought puff pastry
1 egg yolk, lightly beaten

❉ Combine the flour, salt, and pepper in a bowl, then toss the beef in the mixture until evenly coated.

❉ Heat 3 tablespoons of oil in a large skillet over medium-high heat. Cook the beef in batches and transfer to a flameproof casserole dish. Deglaze the skillet with ¼ cup of stock, and add the liquid to the casserole dish.

❉ Heat another 1–2 tablespoons of oil in the skillet and cook the onion and mushrooms for 6–7 minutes, until soft. Add to the casserole dish with the tomato paste, thyme, stout, and remaining stock. Heat the casserole dish over medium-high heat, bring to a boil, then simmer gently with the lid slightly askew for 1½ hours. Check the seasoning.

❉ Drain the meat mixture in a strainer set over a bowl, reserving the liquid. Let rest until cool.

❉ Preheat the oven to 425°F. Put a baking sheet in the oven to heat.

❉ Divide the meat mixture among four individual 1¾-cup pie plates with a flat rim, or ovenproof bowls. Pour in enough liquid so that it doesn't quite cover the filling. Dampen the rims of the pie plates.

❉ Cut the pastry into quarters. Roll out each piece to about 1 inch bigger than the pie plates. From each quarter, cut a ½-inch strip and press it onto a dampened rim. Brush with egg yolk, then drape the pastry quarter on top, covering the strip. Trim, crimp the edges with a fork, and make three slashes down the middle. Decorate the tops with shapes cut from the trimmings. Brush with the remaining egg yolk.

❉ Place the pies on the preheated baking sheet and bake in the preheated oven for 20 minutes. Reduce the heat to 400°F and bake for an additional 5 minutes.

Cockle & Mussel Gratin

Cockles and mussels have always been popular in Irish coastal communities. They could be collected from the shore instead of risking the potential peril of a boat. In this recipe, the two are cooked in a rich and tasty gratin. The crisp topping provides contrasting texture and flavor to the seafood below. If you can't find cockles, use small clams instead.

Serves 3–4

1 3/4 pounds mussels, scrubbed and debearded
1/2 cup water
1/2 cup (1 stick) lightly salted butter
2 onions, chopped
1 1/4 cups cooked shelled cockles
juice and finely grated zest of 1/2 lemon
3 tablespoons chopped fresh parsley
salt and pepper
1 cup coarse bread crumbs from a day-old ciabatta loaf
2 garlic cloves, finely chopped

- Preheat the oven to 425°F. Discard any mussels with broken shells or any that refuse to close when tapped. Put in a large saucepan with the water. Cover and steam for 4–5 minutes, until the shells open. Discard any mussels that remain closed. Reserve eight mussels in their shells as a garnish. Remove the rest from the shells.

- Melt half of the butter in a skillet over medium-high heat. Add the onions and sauté for 7 minutes, until soft but not colored. Transfer to a 2-quart gratin dish.

- Add the cockles, shelled mussels, lemon juice, and 2 tablespoons of the parsley. Season with salt and pepper and stir to mix.

- Set aside a pat of butter and melt the remaining butter. Mix with the bread crumbs, garlic, lemon zest, and remaining parsley. Season with a little more salt and pepper.

- Spread the bread crumb mixture over the seafood. Top with the reserved mussels and dot them with the remaining butter.

- Bake in the oven for 10–15 minutes, until the crumbs are golden and crisp and the seafood is thoroughly heated. Serve immediately.

Fisherman's Pie

TO USE YOUR PIE PAN
Follow the recipe with these changes: use one-third of the fish fillets, wine, and herbs, and bake in the greased pie pan for 15 minutes. Top with one-third of the sautéed mushrooms and one-third of the cooked, peeled shrimp. Make the sauce with 1 tablespoon butter, 1 tablespoon all-purpose flour, the strained cooking liquid and 4 tablespoons heavy cream. Top with 1 pound boiled potatoes, mashed with butter. Place the pie pan on a baking sheet and bake for 10–15 minutes until golden.

Serves 6

- 2 pounds white fish fillets, such as flounder or sole, skinned
- $2/3$ cup dry white wine
- 1 tablespoon chopped fresh parsley, tarragon, or dill
- $2^{1}/_{2}$ cups sliced white button mushrooms
- 7 tablespoons lightly salted butter, plus extra for greasing
- 6 ounces cooked, peeled shrimp
- $1/3$ cup all-purpose flour
- $1/2$ cup heavy cream
- 2 pounds starchy potatoes, such as russets or Yukon Gold, cut into chunks
- salt and pepper

- Preheat the oven to 350°F. Grease a 2-quart baking dish.

- Fold the fish fillets in half and place in the dish. Season well with salt and pepper, add the wine, and sprinkle over the herbs.

- Cover with aluminum foil and bake in the preheated oven for 15 minutes, until the fish starts to flake. Strain off the liquid and reserve for the sauce. Increase the oven temperature to 425°F.

- Heat 1 tablespoon of the butter in a skillet, add the mushrooms, and sauté them for about 5 minutes, or until they are soft and release their juices. Spoon them over the fish, then scatter the shrimp on top

- Heat 4 tablespoons of the remaining butter in a saucepan and stir in the flour. Cook for a few minutes without browning, then remove from the heat and add the reserved cooking liquid gradually, stirring well between each addition.

- Return the pan to the heat and gently bring to a boil, stirring. Add the cream and season to taste with salt and pepper. Pour the sauce over the fish in the dish and smooth over the surface.

- Meanwhile, cook the potatoes in a large saucepan of boiling salted water for 15–20 minutes. Drain well and mash with a potato masher until smooth. Season to taste with salt and pepper and add the remaining butter, stirring until melted.

- Pile or pipe the mashed potato onto the fish and sauce and bake in the preheated oven for 10–15 minutes, until golden brown.

Irish Stew

This robust stew was traditionally made using lamb or mutton (meat from a sheep over a year old), potatoes, onions, and sometimes carrots. It is a white stew, meaning that the meat is not browned. If you can, make it a day in advance so that the delicious flavors have time to blend together.

Serves 4

1/4 cup all-purpose flour
3 pounds neck of lamb, trimmed of visible fat
3 large onions, chopped
3 carrots, sliced
4 starchy potatoes, such as russets, white round, or Yukon Gold, quartered
1/2 teaspoon dried thyme
3 1/2 cups hot beef stock
salt and pepper
2 tablespoons chopped fresh parsley, to garnish

- Preheat the oven to 325°F. Put the flour in a plastic bag and season well with salt and pepper. Add the lamb to the bag, tie the top, and shake well to coat. Do this in batches if necessary. Arrange the lamb in the bottom of a casserole dish.
- Layer the onions, carrots, and potatoes on top of the lamb.
- Sprinkle in the thyme and pour in the stock, then cover and cook in the preheated oven for 2 1/2 hours. Garnish with the parsley and serve straight from the casserole dish.

COBH HARBOUR, COUNTY CORK

Potato, Leek & Chicken Pie

TO USE YOUR PIE PAN
Follow the recipe with these changes: use half quantities of the filling ingredients and spoon the mixture into the pie pan. Do not line it with pastry. Melt 2 tablespoons butter and brush a little on the rim of the dish. Top the pie filling with 3 sheets phyllo pastry brushed with the rest of the melted butter. Bake for 30-35 minutes until the pastry is crisp and golden.

Serves 4

2 waxy potatoes, such as russets, cubed
7 tablespoons lightly salted butter
1 skinless, boneless chicken breast, about 6 ounces, cubed
1 leek, sliced
2 cups sliced cremini mushrooms
2$\frac{1}{2}$ tablespoons all-purpose flour
1$\frac{1}{4}$ cups milk
1 tablespoon Dijon mustard
2 tablespoons chopped fresh sage
8 ounces phyllo pastry, thawed if frozen
salt and pepper

- Preheat the oven to 350°F. Cook the potatoes in a saucepan of boiling water for 5 minutes. Drain and set aside.

- Melt half of the butter in a skillet and cook the chicken for 5 minutes, or until browned all over.

- Add the leek and mushrooms and cook for 3 minutes, stirring. Stir in the flour and cook for 1 minute, stirring continuously. Gradually stir in the milk and bring to a boil. Add the mustard, sage, and potatoes, season to taste with salt and pepper, and simmer for 10 minutes.

- Meanwhile, melt the remaining butter in a small saucepan. Line a deep pie pan with half of the sheets of phyllo pastry. Spoon the chicken mixture into the dish and cover with a sheet of pastry. Brush the pastry with a little of the melted butter and lay another sheet on top. Brush this sheet with melted butter.

- Cut the remaining phyllo pastry into strips and fold them onto the top of the pie to create a ruffled effect. Brush the strips with the remaining melted butter and cook in the preheated oven for 45 minutes, or until golden brown and crisp. Serve hot.

# Dublin Coddle

This nourishing and economical dish of bacon, sausage, and potatoes has been a favorite in Ireland, particularly in Dublin, since the seventeenth century. It is invariably served with soda bread to mop up the juices, which, if the dish has been properly "coddled," or slow-cooked, should be thick.

Serves 4–6

1 pound bacon strips
8 good-quality pork sausages
4 onions, sliced
black pepper
1 leek, some green tops included, sliced
2 bay leaves
2 sprigs thyme
¼ cup chopped fresh parsley
2 garlic cloves, chopped
6 starchy potatoes, such as russets, peeled and cut into 2 or 3 large chunks
3 cups ham stock or chicken stock
soda bread, to serve

✻ Preheat the broiler to high and preheat the oven to 300°F. Broil the bacon for 7–8 minutes, until just starting to crisp. Drain on paper towels, slice in half widthwise, and set aside. Reserve the fat in the broiler pan.

✻ Heat a skillet over medium heat, add the sausages, and cook, turning, for about 15 minutes, until evenly browned. If necessary, use a little bacon fat to prevent the sausages from sticking. Remove the sausages from the skillet, slice in half widthwise, and set aside.

✻ Using the sausage skillet, gently cook the onions for 7 minutes, until soft but not colored. Add more bacon fat if necessary.

✻ Layer the onions, sausages, and bacon in the bottom of a flameproof casserole dish, seasoning each layer with plenty of black pepper. Add the leek, herbs, and garlic, and finish with a layer of potatoes. Season with a little more black pepper, then pour in the stock.

✻ Cover the casserole dish tightly and bring to a boil on top of the stove. Transfer to the preheated oven and cook for 45 minutes, or until the potatoes are tender.

✻ Serve with chunks of soda bread to mop up the juices.

Roast Goose with Apple Stuffing & Cider Gravy

In days gone by, it was customary in Ireland to eat a young goose on Michelmas Day (September 29). According to Irish folklore, doing so provided protection from financial hardship. Michaelmas also coincided with the apple harvest—hence the tradition of an apple-based stuffing, as in this recipe, and applesauce as an accompaniment.

Serves 4–5

1 x 8¾-pound goose, with the giblets (the neck, heart, and gizzard) and lumps of fat in the cavity reserved, and wingtips and leg tips cut off and reserved
1 onion, coarsely chopped
1 celery stalk, coarsely chopped
1 large carrot, coarsely chopped
handful of parsley
2–3 thyme sprigs
2 fresh bay leaves
½ teaspoon black peppercorns
2 small firm apples
1 cup hard dry cider
2 tablespoons apple cider vinegar
2 tablespoons all-purpose flour
salt and pepper

Apple stuffing
1 tablespoon goose fat
3 onions, chopped
4 unsmoked bacon strips, chopped
4 starchy potatoes, such as russets, peeled and cut into ½-inch dice
3 cooking apples, such as Granny Smith or Gravenstein, quartered, cored, peeled, and coarsely chopped
1½ tablespoons chopped fresh sage
1 tablespoon chopped fresh thyme
½ teaspoon sea salt
¼ teaspoon black pepper
4 ounces goose liver, chopped
2 tablespoons chopped fresh parsley
finely grated zest of 1 lemon

❊ Prick the goose all over with a fork and place in a colander. Douse with plenty of boiling water, then pat dry with paper towels. Season inside the cavity with salt and pepper, and rub salt all over the skin. Let dry.

❊ To make the stuffing, heat a pat of goose fat in a skillet over medium heat, add the onion, and cook until soft. Add the bacon, potatoes, apples, sage, thyme, salt, and pepper. Gently cook, covered, for 20 minutes, until the apples are soft. Add the liver, parsley, and lemon zest, and cook for 5 minutes. Spread out the stuffing in a wide bowl and let cool.

❊ Meanwhile, make a stock. Put the reserved wing and leg tips and giblets in a saucepan. Add the vegetables, herbs, and peppercorns. Pour in enough cold water to just cover. Slowly bring to a boil, covered, reduce the heat, and simmer with the lid askew for 2 hours.

❊ Preheat the oven to 400°F. Spoon the stuffing into the goose cavity. Insert a small apple at each end to hold the stuffing in place, then seal the flaps with toothpicks. Truss the wings and legs with twine. Put the goose in a roasting pan and cook for 30 minutes, then pour off the fat. Reduce the temperature to 350°F. Cover the goose loosely with aluminum foil and cook for 1½ hours, pouring off the fat twice again at 30-minute intervals. Add a little water if the pan looks dry. Remove the foil and roast for 30 minutes, until the juices run clear when the thickest part of the thigh is pierced with a sharp knife. Lift the goose onto a warm platter, cover with foil, and let rest for 20 minutes.

❊ To make the gravy, strain 2 cups of stock and blot up any fat that rises. Pour off the fat from the roasting pan. Stir in the cider and vinegar, heat over medium heat, scraping up any sediment in the pan. Add the flour and stir for a minute, until blended. Pour in the strained stock. Bring to a boil, simmer for 5 minutes, and strain.

❊ Slice the apples and arrange around the goose. Carve the goose and serve with the sliced apples, stuffing, and cider gravy.

Winter Vegetable Cobbler

While a cobbler can be a fruit dessert similar to a crisp, any cobbler dish found on the menu in an Irish pub is more likely to be a main course or side dish, not a dessert. Cobblers are typically meat stews topped with thick circles of a biscuit-like dough, with each circle forming a separate "cobble." This is a vegetarian version.

Serves 4

1 tbsp olive oil
1 garlic clove, crushed
8 small onions, halved
2 celery stalks, sliced
2 carrots, sliced
1 3/4 cups chopped rutabaga (if available)
1/2 small cauliflower, broken into florets
3 cups sliced mushrooms
1 2/3 cups of canned chopped tomatoes
1/4 cup red lentils
2 tablespoons cornstarch
3–4 tablespoons water
1 1/4 cups vegetable stock
2 teaspoons Tabasco sauce
2 teaspoons chopped fresh oregano, plus extra sprigs to garnish

Cobbler topping

1 3/4 cups all-purpose flour
2 1/2 teaspoons baking powder
1 teaspoon salt
4 tablespoons lightly salted butter
1 cup shredded sharp cheddar cheese
2 teaspoons chopped fresh oregano
1 egg, lightly beaten
2/3 cup milk

- Preheat the oven to 350°F. Heat the oil in a large flameproof casserole dish over medium heat, add the garlic and onions, and cook for 5 minutes, until softened. Add the celery, carrots, rutabaga, and cauliflower, and cook for 2–3 minutes. Add the mushrooms, tomatoes, and lentils. Mix together the cornstarch and water and stir into the casserole with the stock, Tabasco, and chopped oregano.

- Cover the casserole dish, then transfer to the preheated oven and bake for 20 minutes.

- To make the cobbler topping, sift the flour, baking powder, and salt into a bowl. Rub in the butter, then stir in most of the cheese and the chopped oregano. Beat the egg with the milk and add enough of the mixture to the dry ingredients to make a soft dough. Knead lightly, roll out to a thickness of 1/2 inch and cut into 2-inch circles.

- Remove the dish from the oven and increase the temperature to 400°F. Arrange the dough circles around the edge of the dish, brush with the remaining egg and milk, and sprinkle with the reserved cheese. Cook for an additional 10–12 minutes, or until the topping is golden brown. Garnish with oregano sprigs and serve.

Chapter 3
SIDES

# Irish Soda Bread

Soda bread has long been a staple in Ireland. It is a bread made without yeast, because baking soda mixed with buttermilk is used as a leavening agent. A cross is cut into the top of the bread to help it rise and, according to Irish folklore, to either ward off evil or let the fairies out.

Makes 1 loaf

vegetable oil, for oiling
3²⁄₃ cups all-purpose flour, plus extra for dusting
1 teaspoon salt
1 teaspoon baking soda
1³⁄₄ cups buttermilk

❈ Preheat the oven to 425°F. Oil a baking sheet.

❈ Sift the flour, salt, and baking soda into a mixing bowl. Make a well in the center and pour in most of the buttermilk. Mix together well using your hands. The dough should be soft but not too wet. If necessary, add the remaining buttermilk.

❈ Turn the dough out onto a lightly floured surface and knead it lightly. Shape into an 8-inch circle. Place the loaf on the prepared baking sheet and cut a cross into the top with a sharp knife.

❈ Bake in the preheated oven for 25–30 minutes, until golden brown and it sounds hollow when tapped on the bottom. Transfer to a wire rack and let cool slightly. Serve warm.

TRIM CASTLE, COUNTY MEATH

Boxty Bread

The Irish have always been adept at baking, making do with the simplest of ingredients and equipment. This traditional bread is made with potato and wheat flour dough, shaped into flat circles. It makes a delicious afternoon snack served warm with plenty of butter or cheese and pickles.

Makes 4 small loaves

7 starchy potatoes (about 1¾ pounds), such as russets or Yukon Gold
2 tablespoons lightly salted butter, plus extra to serve
⅔ cup milk
2 teaspoons salt
½ teaspoon black pepper
1½ teaspoons dill seeds or caraway seeds (optional)
2¾ cups all-purpose flour, plus extra for dusting
5 teaspoons baking powder

❈ Preheat the oven to 375°F. Peel four of the potatoes, cut them into even chunks, and bring to a boil in a large saucepan of salted water. Cover and simmer gently for about 20 minutes, until tender. Drain well and put back in the pan. Cover with a clean dish towel for a few minutes to get rid of excess moisture. Mash with the butter until smooth.

❈ Meanwhile, peel the remaining three potatoes and grate coarsely. Wrap in a clean piece of cheesecloth and squeeze tightly to remove the moisture. Put the grated potatoes in a large bowl with the milk, ¾ teaspoon of the salt, the pepper, and dill seeds, if using. Beat in the mashed potatoes.

❈ Sift the flour, baking powder, and remaining salt onto the potato mixture. Mix to a smooth dough, adding a little more flour if the mixture is too soft.

❈ Knead lightly, then shape into four flat, round loaves about 4 inches in diameter. Place on a nonstick baking sheet. Mark each loaf with a large cross. Bake in the preheated oven for 40 minutes, or until well-risen and golden brown.

❈ Break each loaf into quarters. Serve warm, spread with butter.

Sticky Carrots with Whiskey & Ginger Glaze

Comforting carrots take on a new lease of life sizzled in butter with snippets of ginger. The juices reduce to a delicious syrupy glaze, while a glug of whiskey gives the dish an Irish touch.

Serves 2–3

1 teaspoon sugar
½ teaspoon black pepper
good pinch of sea salt flakes
¼ cup peanut oil
3 tablespoons lightly salted butter
4 large carrots (about 1 pound), diagonally sliced into ½-inch circles
¾-inch piece fresh ginger, sliced into matchstick strips
2 tablespoons Irish whiskey
½ cup chicken stock or vegetable stock

✛ Combine the sugar, pepper, and sea salt and set aside.

✛ Heat the oil and half of the butter in a large skillet. Add the carrots in a single layer and sprinkle with the sugar mixture. Cook over medium-high heat for 3 minutes, then start turning the slices with tongs and reduce the heat if necessary. When slightly browned on both sides and starting to blacken at the edges, transfer the carrots to a plate.

✛ Clean the skillet with paper towels. Add the ginger and cook over medium-high heat for 1–2 minutes, until golden. Add to the carrots.

✛ Add the remaining butter, the whiskey, and stock. Bring to a boil, then simmer for 3 minutes, or until syrupy. Return the carrots and ginger to the skillet, and swirl with the syrup for 1 minute. Serve immediately.

Champ

One of Ireland's most delicious side dishes, champ is made with creamy mashed potatoes mixed with chives or scallions, piled high in a bowl with a pool of melted butter in the center. It was traditionally served at Halloween, when it was customary to leave a bowl under a bush for the fairies.

Serves 4

8 starchy potatoes (about 2 pounds), such as russets or Yukon Gold, peeled and cut into even chunks
20 scallions, some green tops included, chopped
1½ cups milk
¼ teaspoon white peppercorns
¼ cup snipped chives
1 teaspoon sea salt flakes
½ cup (1 stick) lightly salted butter, melted and hot

❉ Add the potatoes to a large saucepan of salted boiling water, cover, bring back to a boil, and simmer gently for 20 minutes, until tender. Drain well and put back in the pan. Cover with a clean dish towel for a few minutes to get rid of excess moisture.

❉ While the potatoes are cooking, put the chopped scallions in a saucepan with the milk and peppercorns. Simmer for 5 minutes, then drain, reserving the milk and scallions separately.

❉ Mash the potatoes until smooth, stirring in enough of the reserved milk to produce a creamy consistency. Stir in the scallions and chives. Season to taste with sea salt flakes and more pepper if necessary.

❉ Transfer the potato mixture to a warm serving dish. Make a well in the center and pour in the hot, melted butter. Serve immediately, mixing in the melted butter at the table.

Roasted Banana Shallots with Bread Crumbs & Cheddar

A stalwart of Irish cuisine, onions take pride of place in this tasty gratin. Topped with crisp bread crumbs and Irish cheddar cheese, the dish is equally suitable as a vegetarian main course or an accompaniment to roast beef or lamb.

Serves 4–6

8 banana shallots or small-to-medium onions
2 tablespoons apple juice concentrate
6 tablespoons olive oil or canola oil
$1/2$ tablespoon finely chopped fresh thyme or rosemary
$1/4$ teaspoon black pepper
sea salt flakes
$2/3$ cup coarse stale bread crumbs
1 cup shredded mild Irish cheddar cheese
1 tablespoon chopped fresh parsley, to garnish

※ Preheat the oven to 425°F. Peel the banana shallots, slice in half lengthwise, and put in a shallow bowl.

※ Whisk together the apple juice concentrate, 4 tablespoons of the olive oil, and the thyme. Pour the mixture over the shallots, turning to coat well.

※ Transfer the contents of the bowl into a small nonstick roasting pan in which the shallots fit in a single layer. Turn the shallots cut-side up and season with the pepper and a good pinch of sea salt flakes. Sprinkle with the bread crumbs and the remaining oil.

※ Roast in the preheated oven for 25–30 minutes, or until the shallots are soft and the edges are beginning to blacken. Scatter the shredded cheese over the top, and roast for an additional 3 minutes, or until the cheese is melted and bubbling.

※ Garnish with the parsley and serve immediately.

Buttered Kale with Chives & Lemon

Kale is a sturdy crop that features regularly on the Irish menu, particularly in winter. In this recipe, it is lightly cooked and seasoned with lemon zest and chives to complement the rich and earthy flavor.

Serves 4–6

8 ounces kale
grated zest of 1 lemon
⅓ cup snipped chives
large pat of lightly salted butter
sea salt flakes
white pepper

❋ Remove the tough stems from the kale, then stack the leaves and slice into wide ribbons. Place in a steamer basket set over boiling water. Steam for 10–12 minutes, until tender but still bright green.

❋ Transfer the kale to a warm serving dish, add the lemon zest, chives, and butter, and toss together. Season with sea salt flakes and pepper. Serve immediately.

TRADITIONAL HOUSE, COUNTY WICKLOW

Red Cabbage with Mushrooms, Nuts & Bacon

A major feature of Irish cuisine, cabbage comes in a range of appetizing colors and flavors. In this recipe, red cabbage is lightly braised with bacon, mushrooms, and crunchy nuts and is a superb accompaniment to roast goose or pork.

Serves 4

1/2 large red cabbage
2 tbsp canola oil or vegetable oil
6 thin bacon strips, cut into bite-size pieces
1 onion, chopped
2 teaspoons thyme leaves
2 1/2 cups coarsely chopped cremini mushrooms
1/3 cup toasted hazelnuts, coarsely chopped
grated zest of 1 lemon
1 teaspoon sea salt flakes
1/2 teaspoon black pepper
1/2 teaspoon sugar
2 tablespoons apple cider vinegar
1 cup meat stock
1/4 cup chopped fresh parsley
pat of lightly salted butter

- Quarter the cabbage lengthwise and discard the tough core in the center. Slice the leaves widthwise into ribbons.
- Heat the oil in a flameproof casserole dish or deep skillet over medium-high heat. Add the bacon and cook for about 5 minutes, or until crisp.
- Reduce the heat to medium, add the onion and thyme, and cook for 5 minutes, until the onion is translucent.
- Add the mushrooms and cabbage, and cook for an additional 5 minutes, until starting to soften.
- Stir in the nuts, lemon zest, sea salt, pepper, and sugar, and cook for an additional 3 minutes. Pour in the vinegar and stock, cover, and bring to a boil, then reduce the heat and simmer for 15 minutes, until the cabbage is tender.
- Check the seasoning, adding salt and pepper if necessary. Stir in the parsley and a pat of butter just before serving.

Chapter 4
DESSERTS

Irish Whiskey Trifle

Trifle is said to have a "powerful stronghold" in Ireland, with every family having its favorite recipe that is, of course, better than anyone else's. This version contains the usual Irish whiskey and sherry, but you could use fruit juice for soaking if you prefer a nonalcoholic version.

Serves 8

10 ladyfingers or 1 stale sponge cake
raspberry jam, for spreading
2 macaroons, lightly crushed
finely grated zest of 1 lemon
2 tablespoons Irish whiskey
½ cup sherry
1¼ cups heavy cream
½ tablespoon sugar
1 cup raspberries
candied violets or miniature macaroons, to decorate

Custard

5 egg yolks, lightly beaten
¼ cup sugar
2 teaspoons cornstarch
½ cup whole milk
1 cup heavy cream
½ teaspoon vanilla extract

- First make the custard. Combine the egg yolks and sugar in a mixing bowl. Stir in the cornstarch and mix to a smooth paste, then whisk in the milk.

- Heat the cream in a heavy saucepan until just starting to simmer but not boiling. Gradually whisk the hot cream into the egg mixture, then return the mixture to the pan. Whisk continuously over medium heat for about 5 minutes, until thickened. Immediately pour into a pitcher and stir in the vanilla extract. Cover with plastic wrap to prevent a skin from forming and let stand to cool completely.

- Thickly spread half of the ladyfingers with raspberry jam. Place the remaining ladyfingers on top to make a sandwich. If using sponge cake, slice horizontally into two or three layers and spread with jam. Arrange in a single layer in the bottom of a deep serving dish. Sprinkle with the crushed macaroons and the lemon zest.

- Combine the whiskey and sherry and pour over the ladyfinger mixture. Let soak for 1 hour.

- Spoon the cooled custard over the ladyfinger mixture.

- Whip the cream with the sugar until stiff peaks form. Spread over the custard, leveling with a spatula. Cover with plastic wrap and chill for 1 hour, or until ready to serve.

- Arrange the raspberries on top and decorate with candied violets or miniature macaroons.

Chocolate & Stout Ice Cream

This extremely rich, dark ice cream is perfect for a St. Patrick's Day celebration. Served cold, the stout flavor is subtle and perfectly matched by dark, bittersweet chocolate. For an extra-special touch, splash a little Irish cream liqueur over each serving.

Makes about 3½ cups

1½ cups whole milk
¾ cup sugar
5½ ounces semisweet chocolate (at least 85 percent cocoa solids), broken into small pieces
4 egg yolks
1 teaspoon vanilla extract
1⅓ cups stout
1 cup heavy cream
grated chocolate, to decorate

- Pour the milk into a saucepan and add the sugar. Bring to a boil, stirring, until the sugar has dissolved. Remove from the heat and stir in the chocolate.

- Pour the egg yolks into a heatproof bowl and beat for 5 minutes, or until the beaters leave a faint trail when lifted from the mixture. Stir some of the warm chocolate mixture into the egg yolks, then gradually beat in the rest.

- Place the bowl over a saucepan of gently boiling water. Stir continuously for about 10 minutes, until the mixture reaches a temperature of 185°F, or is thick enough to coat the back of a spoon. Be careful not to let it boil.

- Strain the mixture through a fine strainer into a pitcher. Stir in the vanilla extract. Sit the bottom of the pitcher in iced water until cold, then cover with plastic wrap and chill for 2 hours.

- Meanwhile, pour the stout into a saucepan and bring to a boil. Reduce the heat and simmer briskly for 8 minutes, until reduced to 1 cup. Pour into a pitcher, let cool, then chill in the refrigerator.

- Stir the cream and chilled stout into the chocolate mixture, mixing well. Pour the mixture into the bowl of an ice-cream machine. Churn and freeze following the manufacturer's instructions. Alternatively, pour the mixture into a shallow freezer-proof container, cover with plastic wrap, and freeze for about 2 hours, until beginning to harden around the edges. Beat until smooth to get rid of any ice crystals. Freeze again, repeat the process twice, then freeze until completely firm.

- Move the ice cream to the refrigerator to soften 30 minutes before serving. Serve in chilled dishes, sprinkled with grated chocolate.

Porter Cake

Porter, or stout, is a special type of dark beer first brewed in Ireland in the eighteenth century. Guinness is an extra-strong porter that provides color and flavor without being too overwhelming. Stored in an airtight container, this rich, moist fruitcake is best eaten several days after baking.

Makes one 7-inch cake

3 cups mixed currants and golden raisins
1 cup dried unsweetened cherries
3/4 cup finely chopped candied citrus peel
1 1/3 cups stout
2 3/4 cups all-purpose flour
1 teaspoon baking powder
1 teaspoon allspice
pinch of salt
1 cup (2 sticks) butter
1 cup firmly packed brown sugar
3 eggs, lightly beaten

- Mix the currants, golden raisins, cherries, and citrus peel in a large bowl. Add the stout and let soak for at least 5 hours or overnight, stirring occasionally.
- Preheat the oven to 325°F. Grease and line a 7-inch square cake pan.
- Sift the flour, baking powder, spice, and salt into a large bowl.
- Cream the butter and sugar in a separate bowl for about 4 minutes, until light and fluffy. Stir in the beaten eggs, a little at a time, adding some of the flour mixture at each addition and beating well. Stir in the remaining flour.
- Add the fruit and any liquid to the batter, mixing well to a soft consistency. Spoon the batter into the prepared pan, leveling the surface with a wet spatula.
- Bake in the preheated oven for 1 hour. Reduce the oven temperature to 300°F and bake for an additional 1 1/2–2 hours, or until a toothpick inserted in the center comes out clean. Let rest in the pan until completely cool.
- Invert, wrap in wax paper, and store in an airtight container.

Oatmeal & Raspberry Cream

Oats became important to the Irish during the potato famine in the mid-nineteenth century. In this recipe, they are folded into an irresistible concoction of raspberries and whiskey-and honey-flavored cream. The dish was traditionally served to celebrate the end of the annual harvest. It is rich, so the portions are small.

Serves 6

1 cup rolled oats
1½ cups heavy cream
½ cup light cream
3 tablespoons Irish whiskey
2 tablespoons honey,
 plus extra for drizzling
2½ cups raspberries

❋ Preheat the broiler to medium. Spread out the oats on a baking sheet, place under the preheated broiler, and toast for 4–5 minutes, or until golden brown, stirring often to prevent burning. Transfer to a shallow bowl and let cool.

❋ Combine the two creams, whiskey, and honey in a mixing bowl. Stir in the oats, mixing well. Cover with plastic wrap and let rest in the refrigerator for at least 2 hours or overnight to thicken. Stir occasionally to break up any clumps of oats.

❋ Set aside ⅓ cup of the best raspberries to decorate. Lightly swirl the remaining raspberries into the oat mixture, creating attractive pink streaks. Spoon into glass serving dishes and decorate with the reserved raspberries. Drizzle with honey just before serving.

Irish Cream Cheesecake

This is an unbaked cheesecake and, although it contains no gelatin, its high chocolate content guarantees that it sets perfectly. It is a luxurious dessert that is made even more special by the addition of Irish cream, a popular liqueur made from Irish whiskey, coffee, and cream.

Serves 8

vegetable oil, for oiling
4 tablespoons unsalted butter
1½ cups crushed chocolate chip cookies
crème fraîche or whipped cream and fresh strawberries, to serve

Filling

8 ounces semisweet dark chocolate, broken into pieces
8 ounces milk chocolate, broken into pieces
¼ cup sugar
1½ cups cream cheese
2 cups heavy cream, lightly whipped
3 tablespoons Irish cream liqueur

❊ Line the bottom of an 8-inch round springform cake pan with parchment paper and brush the sides with oil. Put the butter in a saucepan and heat gently until melted. Stir in the crushed cookies. Press into the bottom of the prepared cake pan and chill in the refrigerator for 1 hour.

❊ To make the filling, put the dark and milk chocolates into a heatproof bowl set over a saucepan of gently simmering water until melted. Let cool. Put the sugar and cream cheese in a bowl and beat together until smooth, then fold in the cream. Fold the melted chocolate into the cream cheese mixture, then stir in the liqueur.

❊ Spoon into the cake pan and smooth the surface. Let chill in the refrigerator for 2 hours, or until firm. Transfer to a serving plate and cut into slices. Serve with crème fraîche and strawberries.

Index

apples
　Roast Goose with Apple Stuffing &
　　Cider Gravy 33

bacon
　Bacon, Beet & Spinach Salad with
　　Cashel Blue Cheese 16
　Dublin Coddle 30
　Red Cabbage with Mushrooms, Nuts
　　& Bacon 50
　Beef & Stout Pies 20
beetroot
　Bacon, Beet & Spinach Salad with
　　Cashel Blue Cheese 16
Boxty Bread 40
bread
　Boxty Bread 40
　Cockle & Mussel Gratin 23
　Irish Rarebit 13
　Irish Soda Bread 38
　Roasted Banana Shallots with Bread
　　Crumbs & Cheddar 46
　Buttered Kale with Chives & Lemon 49
buttermilk
　Irish Buttermilk Pancakes 8

cabbage
　Red Cabbage with Mushrooms, Nuts
　　& Bacon 50
carrots
　Sticky Carrots with Whiskey & Ginger
　　Glaze 43
Champ 44
cheese
　Bacon, Beet & Spinach Salad with
　　Cashel Blue Cheese 16
　Irish Rarebit 13
　Roasted Banana Shallots with Bread
　　Crumbs & Cheddar 46
cheesecake
　Irish Cream Cheesecake 62
chicken
　Potato, Leek & Chicken Pie 29
　Skink Soup 10
chives
　Buttered Kale with Chives &
　　Lemon 49
chocolate
　Chocolate & Stout Ice Cream 56
　Irish Cream Cheesecake 62
cider
　Roast Goose with Apple Stuffing &
　　Cider Gravy 33
cobbler topping 35
Cockle & Mussel Gratin 23
cream
　Chocolate & Stout Ice Cream 56
　Irish Cream Cheesecake 62
　Irish Whiskey Trifle 54
　Oatmeal & Raspberry Cream 60

custard
　Irish Whiskey Trifle 54

dried fruit
　Porter Cake 58
　Dublin Coddle 30

fish
　Fisherman's Pie 24
　Kipper & Potato Salad with Mustard
　　Dressing 14

ginger
　Sticky Carrots with Whiskey & Ginger
　　Glaze 43
goose
　Roast Goose with Apple Stuffing &
　　Cider Gravy 33

herring
　Kipper & Potato Salad with Mustard
　　Dressing 14

ice cream
　Chocolate & Stout Ice Cream 56
　Irish Buttermilk Pancakes 8
　Irish Cream Cheesecake 62
　Irish Rarebit 13
　Irish Soda Bread 38
　Irish Stew 26
　Irish Whiskey Trifle 54

kale
　Buttered Kale with Chives &
　　Lemon 49
　Kipper & Potato Salad with Mustard
　　Dressing 14

lamb
　Irish Stew 26
leeks
　Potato, Leek & Chicken Pie 29
lemons
　Buttered Kale with Chives &
　　Lemon 49

mushrooms
　Beef & Stout Pies 20
　Fisherman's Pie 24
　Red Cabbage with Mushrooms, Nuts
　　& Bacon 50
mussels
　Cockle & Mussel Gratin 23
mustard
　Kipper & Potato Salad with Mustard
　　Dressing 14

nuts
　Red Cabbage with Mushrooms, Nuts
　　& Bacon 50

oats
　Oatmeal & Raspberry Cream 60
onions
　Roasted Banana Shallots with Bread
　　Crumbs & Cheddar 46

Porter Cake 58
potatoes
　Boxty Bread 40
　Champ 44
　Dublin Coddle 30
　Fisherman's Pie 24
　Irish Stew 26
　Kipper & Potato Salad with Mustard
　　Dressing 14
　Potato, Leek & Chicken Pie 29

raspberries
　Irish Whiskey Trifle 54
　Oatmeal & Raspberry Cream 60
　Red Cabbage with Mushrooms, Nuts &
　　Bacon 50
　Roast Goose with Apple Stuffing &
　　Cider Gravy 33
　Roasted Banana Shallots with Bread
　　Crumbs & Cheddar 46

sausage
　Dublin Coddle 30
scallions
　Champ 44
seafood
　Cockle & Mussel Gratin 23
　Fisherman's Pie 24
shallots
　Roasted Banana Shallots with Bread
　　Crumbs & Cheddar 46
Skink Soup 10
spinach
　Bacon, Beet & Spinach Salad with
　　Cashel Blue Cheese 16
　Sticky Carrots with Whiskey & Ginger
　　Glaze 43
stout
　Beef & Stout Pies 20
　Chocolate & Stout Ice Cream 56
　Porter Cake 58

vegetables
　Skink Soup 10
　Winter Vegetable Cobbler 35

whiskey
　Irish Whiskey Trifle 54
　Oatmeal & Raspberry Cream 60
　Sticky Carrots with Whiskey & Ginger
　　Glaze 43
　Winter Vegetable Cobbler 35